The ABCs of Life and Messages for the Soul

JUSTIN SIMMONS

LIVE BY THE WORD:
The ABCs of Life and Messages for the Soul

Copyright © 2024 by Justin Simmons

Definitions are from Merriam-Webster Online Dictionary
copyright © 2012 by Merriam-Webster, Incorporated.
https://www.merriam-webster.com (1 January 2023).

Cover, Layout, & Book Development:
Raindrop Creative, Inc.

Editor: Tiara Brown

ISBN: 978-1-970179-12-5

TABLE OF CONTENT

INTRODUCTION

Thank you so much for entrusting this devotional to be a part of your spiritual journey with God. I must admit that writing this was part of a spiritual cleansing for me because it was born out of pain. While the concepts and topics adjusted over time, I realized I needed to do something when I started to blame the Holy One for my mother's death. Yes, a preacher's kid who grew up in church blamed, questioned, and despised God for two years because I believed the Almighty allowed my mom to experience a slow and agonizing death.

If I'm being transparent, my spiritual relationship was unhealthy. I viewed the Creator as one who rewarded people for their faith and work. And since I knew my mother leaned heavily on her beliefs, it went against everything I had felt and thought I knew. Additionally, my faith diminished quicker than I had imagined because my prayers for my mother's healing went unanswered.

Where do you go when your faith is fractured? I went to everything but the One. However, at my core, I still knew God was present. Therefore, I continued to express my displeasure in the most unpleasant ways possible. It wasn't until one of my rants took a turn for the worse that I heard a quiet voice ask, "What haven't I done for you? I may have taken your mother, but I gave you everything you wanted. You wanted her to have peace, and she gained it. You didn't want her to suffer anymore, and she isn't. You also knew her deepest desire, and it was granted to her. So again, what haven't I done?" I was shocked, and all I could say was, "You're right."

From that moment on, I started seeking a more authentic relationship with God. I no longer relied solely on someone else's interpretation. Instead, I honored my experiences, and the Scriptures centered around Jesus. I also addressed the questions I still had about my beliefs. In turn, I was able to challenge my assumptions, discover my identity, and become empowered throughout the entire process. Hence the creation of this devotional.

During my journey, I focused on studying the Gospels (Matthew, Mark, Luke, and John) and turned to specific words that improved my relationship with Christ. Everyone's relationship with the Master differs, so utilizing words that spoke to my walk with the Savior was paramount. Therefore, at the end of the devotional, you can select words you feel are more appropriate if you disagree with the ones I have chosen.

Each devotional comes with a word, its definition, a poem, the message, and a way to interact with the text, including the four R's: Restore, Reflect, Respond, and Reclaim. The poems illustrate the messages uniquely and entertainingly, while the messages allow personal discovery and empowerment through the Lord's Word. The four R's also ensure we actively participate in our learning or reaffirming. For example, "Restore" can be seen as a reminder of the message. "Reflect" is a question that requires a thought-out answer. "Respond" serves as a task to complete, and "Reclaim" is a prayer to say throughout the day.

Lastly, I am not a licensed preacher or minister, so I may not have the degrees or language that demonstrate an expansive knowledge of God's Word. Yet, I believe in the life-changing power of Jesus Christ, and I strongly desire to deepen my (and the world's) relationship with the Divine. To say that I am excited about what you will experience while you read this devotional is an understatement. I pray you can examine who you are and what you believe and find empowerment through the content of each message while getting closer to God. I am thrilled to be in this process with you, and I hope it blesses you as much as it has me.

With love,
Justin Simmons

CHAPTER 1:
ACCOUNTABILITY

Definition:
An obligation or willingness to accept responsibility or to account for one's actions.

A RACE WITH TIME

*I never knew how great Time was
until we had the meet.
I figured Time would push me
to extraordinary feats.*

*Time adjusted my two blocks
which impacted my start.
I thought I had it all resolved,
and Time said, "Do your part."*

*Not freezing under pressure;
some would say I felt the heat.
Even though there were some hurdles,
I kept landing on my feet.*

*I learned accountability;
Time kept me in my lane.
There was nothing that could stop me
when I gained this needed change.*

WHAT'S THE ISSUE?

(Read Luke 8:43-47)

Scripture spotlight:

"Then the woman, seeing that she could not go unnoticed, came trembling and fell at His feet. In the presence of all the people, she told why she had touched Him and how she had been instantly healed."
— Luke 8:47

L et's be honest. It is easier to hold someone else accountable for something than it is for us to meet the same standard. Our anonymity may aid us in this, but we must understand one thing: we are not anonymous to God. God expects us to accept responsibility for our words and actions.

We see this in the story of the woman with the issue of blood. While we do not know much about her, the text tells us that she spent everything she had on physicians to heal her for twelve years. However, no one could. But consider this: what would have happened if Jesus was her first option?

Now, let us ask ourselves the same question. What would happen to our issues if Jesus was our first option? When we think about it, we are just like this woman. We try to handle our problems and often reach out to Jesus only when desperate. Although Jesus accepts us whenever we reach out to Him, He should never be our last resort. So, we should hold ourselves accountable and change our approach.

The woman realized this when she was healed immediately by touching the hem of Jesus' garment (v. 44). Yet, the interesting thing is that Jesus made an effort to ask, "Who touched me?" (v. 45) when He already knew who did. Was it a test? We may never know, but all denied touching Him. Even Peter, one of His disciples, shared how difficult it would be to identify the individual when the crowd was pressed against Him.

Nevertheless, the woman came trembling toward Jesus when she could no longer stay hidden. She fell before Him, confessed, and explained her reasoning for all to hear. In short, the woman was accountable for her actions, and Jesus did not punish her. He said, "Daughter, be of good cheer; your faith has made you well. Go in peace" (v. 48).

The fascinating piece is that her response was not for selfish gain. Remember, she had already received the blessing, so why did she have to identify herself? She did not, but her confession was for the glorification of God. All who were there encountered Jesus' love and mercy firsthand and could spread the Good News of Jesus Christ in their future interactions. For this reason alone, let us model this woman's accountability so everyone we meet can witness the power of God through our life experiences.

RESTORE

Time will always be there to assist you with being accountable.

_____

_____

_____

REFLECT

What is holding me back from accepting responsibility and trusting God with the outcome?

_____

_____

_____

RESPOND

Think about a time when God held you accountable for your actions. Share that experience with someone and how God responded to you accepting responsibility.

_____

_____

_____

RECLAIM

Dear Lord, thank You for allowing me to see the importance of accountability. Please give me the strength to hold myself accountable even when I do not want to. In Jesus' name, Amen!

_____

_____

_____

CHAPTER 2:
BALANCE

Definition:
Mental and emotional steadiness.

THE DEBATE

"What are you doing with me?"
Life finally asked.
"If Worry always consumes you,
then you won't be able to last."

Worry said that it disagreed
and started with its retort,
"If I'm absent from the picture,
then there's nothing left to court."

Life responded in disbelief,
"Without me, nothing gets done.
Worry can't give you anything
except fear when Worry has won."

Worry had no response for Life,
but knew it had been challenged
of finding ways to exist
when Life maintained its balance.

BALANCING ACT

(Read Matthew 6:25-34)

Scripture spotlight:
"But seek first the kingdom of God and His righteousness, and all these things shall be added to you." – Matthew 6:33

What would it take to attain and maintain balance in our lives? Not the balance where our time is equally distributed, but the one in which our minds are at peace. Due to individuals being multifaceted, the answers may seem complex. Yet, Jesus offers us a simple solution: seek God's kingdom first.

In Matthew 6:25-34, Jesus teaches us not to worry. Why focus on the topic of worry? It could be because He knows the number of self-defeating thoughts, internal debates, and feelings of inadequacy circulating in our minds.

To contend against this, Jesus directs our attention to God by detailing God's provision for the birds of the air and lilies of the field. In these examples, Jesus tells us how the birds are well fed when they neither sow, reap or save and how the lilies are dressed better than the wealthiest man ever to live when they neither toil nor spin (v. 26, 28). During each story, Jesus asks us three questions:

1. Are we not more valuable than these?
2. Will God not do more for us?
3. What will we gain from worrying?

Let us address these questions. And while we reflect on our answers, consider another critical question: why do we worry? Is it because we lack faith?

In verse 30, Jesus certainly seems to think so. He asks, "...O you of little faith?" So, where is our faith? Is it in us because we believe we are the reason for our accomplishments? Is it in others due to being let down or supported by them on multiple occasions? Regardless of where it is, we can agree that our faith is often closely connected to our belief in humans, not God. Therefore, we should acknowledge Jesus' reason for saying, "... seek first the kingdom of God" (v. 33), which is to put our faith in God's power and provision even when we did not earn or deserve it.

Remember, God wants us to live an abundant life, and we cannot do so if we constantly doubt God by worrying. Jesus emphasized this by telling us that God knows what we need and will ultimately provide it. All we need to do is seek God's kingdom first and focus on God's present actions. In doing so, God will handle everything from our pasts, presents, and futures.

RESTORE

Shifting what you seek eliminates the need to worry.

_____

_____

_____

REFLECT

How can I combat worry when it creates a physical, mental, or spiritual imbalance?

_____

_____

_____

RESPOND

Write down things you have been previously worried about and summarize how God's provision showed up in each situation.

_____

_____

_____

RECLAIM

Lord God, I am appreciative of everything You have sent my way. Please help me find the balance needed to worry no longer. In Jesus' name, Amen!

_____

_____

_____

CHAPTER 3:

COMMUNICATION

Definition:
A process by which information is exchanged between individuals through a common system of symbols, signs, or behavior.

COMMUNICATION COUNTS

I guess I must confess,
I'm really easy to define.
Execution may be harder,
but improvement comes with time.

One mistake that people make
is that it's all about them.
The message will be compromised,
and that's my first gem.

Number two is what you do
and rarely what you may say.
Body language, tone, and actions
are a huge giveaway.

Maybe last but not least,
and it's a major piece:
You should listen three times
way more than you speak.

MODEL COMMUNICATION

(Read Matthew 6:5-15)

Scripture spotlight:

"And when you pray, you shall not be like the hypocrites. For they love to pray standing in the synagogues and on the corners of the streets, that they may be seen by men. Assuredly, I say to you, they have their reward." – Matthew 6:5

One of the most important things we can do is communicate. Yet, many of us still need help maintaining and delivering a consistent message because our beliefs, words, and actions are misaligned. However, there is still hope for improvement.

Jesus models this with the Lord's Prayer during His Sermon on the Mount. And since prayer is essential in communicating with God, there are many lessons to learn from Jesus to help us become better communicators—mainly, selflessness.

When Jesus starts His lesson on the Lord's Prayer, He tells us not to be like the hypocrites, for they love to pray to be seen by others (v. 5). If this is the case, we must ask ourselves if we are doing the same thing. How often have we said or done something because we needed to be heard or seen in a particular way? Better yet, how often have we found ourselves thinking about what to say or sharing our own stories as opposed to genuinely listening to the experiences of others?

As we contemplate our answers, notice what Jesus says next. He tells us that our conversations with God should remain private and not offer empty phrases. While examining this, we must determine if we are sharing information about private conversations with others. Also, are we talking without anything to say or being indirect? If so, let us change that. Since we believe God will provide what we need, we can focus our communication on uplifting and caring for one another.

Jesus illustrates this through the remainder of the prayer by using communal language and emphasizing honoring, doing, and relying on God's will. The concluding line of the prayer says, "For Yours is the kingdom and the power and the glory forever. Amen" (v. 13). Given this, we must eliminate what we want and understand what God wants by reading, listening to, and acting on God's Word. Only then will our communication model the kingdom, receive the power, and testify to the glory of God. Therefore, we must continually reflect on this simple question: is God pleased with our communication?

RESTORE

Communication models who you are and what you believe.
Exemplify Godliness.

_____

_____

_____

REFLECT

How will I address my need to become a better communicator?

_____

_____

_____

RESPOND

Honor, converse with, and seek to understand someone with a
different opinion than you.

_____

_____

_____

RECLAIM

Lord, I need You. Please allow the way I communicate to
reflect my beliefs and benefit You, as well as the lives of others.
In Jesus' name, Amen!

_____

_____

_____

CHAPTER 4:
DISCIPLINE

Definition:
Training that corrects, molds, or perfects the mental faculties or moral character.

WORK-IT-OUT

Goals make the plans,
and the plans make you better.
Consistency is key,
and one-hundred percent effort.

Sit up, pull up,
and push your way through,
because fighting for what you want
is way overdue.

The journey is long,
so don't make excuses.
Obstacles, achievements,
and strength it produces.

So discipline yourself,
and celebrate each day.
Persevere through everything
and keep your doubts at bay.

POWERED FROM WITHIN

(Read Luke 10:1-20)

Scripture spotlight:

"After these things the Lord appointed seventy others also, and sent them two by two before His face into every city and place where He Himself was about to go." – Luke 10:1

Staying disciplined is a skill we all have, but only a few employ. And while our failed attempts to follow through can be attributed to many things, we must recognize what is holding us back: ourselves. When we think about it, we often let our thoughts, feelings, and desires shift our attention from what we need to do to what we want to do. Instead, let us learn from the seventy to discover how to stay disciplined despite adversity.

In Luke 10, we notice that Jesus sends out seventy additional people, "two by two" (v. 1), to places He will eventually visit. Interestingly, Jesus tells them, "The harvest is great, but the laborers are few" (v. 2), so pray for help. If Jesus has given them the power to withstand every challenge and tells them this, what do we think Jesus is telling us?

There are a couple of questions we can ask to discern our answers. What are the outcomes we want, who are the people to bring along to keep us disciplined, and are our prayers aligned with what God desires? After we receive the answers to these questions, there is one more thing to contemplate: are we listening to how God tells us to acquire it?

The seventy did because Jesus gave them detailed instructions on how to be successful and the appropriate responses to give when they met resistance. The seventy did not negotiate with Him or discuss how they thought it should go. They followed His directions and achieved things they never thought were possible.

Are we willing to do the same? Are we ready to submit to what God wants instead of our desires? When the seventy did, they celebrated what they could do in Jesus' name. However, Jesus told them not to rejoice in the power He gave but to delight in knowing their names were written in heaven (v. 20).

Knowing this, we should reconsider what staying disciplined does. Although it allows us to accomplish goals and celebrate our victories, it ultimately enables God to do something within us. Remember that God allowed the seventy to stay disciplined to prepare the way for Jesus, and God will do the same for us. Therefore, are we willing and ready to do the same?

Live by The Word

RESTORE

Discipline yourself for the benefit of others and not just for personal gain.

REFLECT

How will I stay disciplined when my wants and needs are misaligned?

RESPOND

Commit to and do something to get you closer to accomplishing a goal you have consistently avoided.

RECLAIM

Lord, thank You for showing me how to be disciplined. Please align my desires with what You want for my life, and let me stay disciplined even when I face adversity. In Jesus' name, Amen!

CHAPTER 5:
ENGAGEMENT

Definition:
Emotional involvement or commitment.

THE PROPOSAL

From the very first moment
that we've been together,
you have been the one
to be down for whatever.

I knew all my options
and played the cards that I'd been dealt.
I didn't consider folding
or losing all our wealth.

Focusing on the present,
firm in my decision.
There's no turning back
and there are certainly no limits.

I'm going all in.
That's how it must be.
It's time for my bet
on you and me.

ALL IN!

(Read Luke 10:38-42)

Scripture spotlight:

*"And Jesus answered and said to her, "Martha, Martha,
you are worried and troubled about many things.
But one thing is needed, and Mary has chosen the good
part, which will not be taken away from her."*
– Luke 10:41-42

Negotiating how we spend our time is one of the most challenging and frequent things we do. If we are not careful, we will miss out on valuable aspects of life due to self-imposed distractions. Unfortunately, this can create frustrating, overwhelming, or disengaging moments.

Martha experienced this when she invited Jesus into her home. During the visit, Martha served (v. 40) while her sister, Mary, sat at Jesus' feet and listened to Him (v. 39). Given this, a question arises. What would Martha have done if she knew she had limited time with Jesus?

Now, let us examine ourselves. How would we respond if we only had one or two more moments with our loved ones? Would we allow anything to distract us?

When in doubt, let us learn from Martha. Since she was the homeowner (v. 38), she took pride in serving and felt it was her responsibility. However, she was worried and troubled about many things (v. 41), which led her to be distracted by how she showed love through service, so much so that she told Jesus to tell Mary to help her when Mary was engaging with Jesus (v. 40).

How does this relate to us? If we were fully engaged with what we were doing, would we pay attention to what someone else was or was not doing? Additionally, would we be so frustrated that we would ask Jesus to make someone else disengage from Him? If we need help figuring it out, let us look at Jesus' response.

He tells Martha, "But one thing is needed, and Mary has chosen that good part, which will not be taken away from her" (v. 42). Jesus did not say Martha chose something wrong. He pointed out that Mary was engaged with Him, while distractions disengaged Martha.

Therefore, we must understand that Jesus wants us to remain fully engaged with how we interact with Him and the people we value. We must limit our distractions to stay present in cherished moments and eliminate the distractions we create for others when we are worried, troubled, or overwhelmed. If we do this, we will be engaged enough to show others how much they mean to us by the impact our engagement has on their lives.

RESTORE

Living in the moments are the moments worth living.

_____

_____

_____

REFLECT

What can I do to show people that they matter to me?

_____

_____

_____

RESPOND

Spend 30 minutes of the day disconnected from distractions when you are with the people you love.

_____

_____

_____

RECLAIM

Lord, I am grateful for the people You have placed in my life. Please allow me to be more engaged with them daily. In Jesus' name, Amen!

_____

_____

_____

CHAPTER 6:
FAITH

Definition:
Firm belief in something for which there is no proof.

<u>WALK BY FAITH</u>

*I remember the day
that I walked by Faith.
Nothing seemed possible
nor felt safe.*

*It was late.
Failure was controlling my mind.
I was walking without looking,
trying to rewind time.*

*That's when it happened.
Faith tapped me on my shoulder,
whispered in my ear
and told me, "Be bolder.*

*Adjust and walk with purpose,
keep your eyes on the prize,
and believe all things are possible
to maximize."*

WHERE'S THE FAITH?

(Read Matthew 8:5-13)

Scripture spotlight:

"The centurion answered and said, "Lord, I am not worthy that you should come under my roof. But only speak a word, and my servant will be healed."
– Matthew 8:8

We have heard many times before, "Just have faith." While we all do, we must search ourselves to understand how we can anchor and strengthen it. To help with this, let us start by analyzing a time when our faith had wavered.

Do we have a situation in mind? Great. Now, let us explore the following question: what did I rely on during this time? As answers permeate, ask, why did I not have enough faith to trust God fully?

Although our responses may vary, we can agree that our lives will change when we act on unquestionable faith. An example occurred in Capernaum when a centurion pleaded with Jesus to heal his paralyzed servant (Matthew 8:5-13). When Jesus agreed to heal him, the centurion quickly said he was not worthy to have Jesus in his home (v. 8). But by citing previous experiences, the centurion knew his servant would be healed if only Jesus spoke a word (v. 8).

As a result, Jesus "marveled" at the centurion's faith (v. 10). Therefore, we should ask ourselves if Jesus can marvel at our faith. If not, what experiences can we pull from to bolster it?

Let us direct our attention to the servant if our answers must be revised. While there is no information on why or how he was paralyzed, we know it tormented him (v. 6). Which is interesting because the same thing happens to us when our faith is paralyzed and plagued by hardships. However, we should know that situations change, healings occur, and trust improves simply through the faith of the people who love us.

This is evident when Jesus tells the centurion in verse 13, "Go; let it be done for you as you have believed." Subsequently, the servant was healed within the hour, and we can assume that his and the centurion's faith grew exponentially. Since we know this happened for them, what are we willing and ready to trust God with now?

RESTORE

Our faith walk is lonely when we do not include others.

_____

_____

_____

REFLECT

What must happen for me to trust God fully with all things?

_____

_____

_____

RESPOND

Have someone pray over a situation you have been struggling
with and do not stress over it.

_____

_____

_____

RECLAIM

Lord, I need Your help. I have been struggling with what I put
my trust in, and I need and want to trust You more. In Jesus'
name, Amen!

_____

_____

_____

CHAPTER 7:
GENUINENESS

Definition:
Free from hypocrisy or pretense.

THE REAL DEAL

Let's make a deal.
One you shouldn't refuse.
I believe you should do it.
You have nothing to lose.

The deal is being genuine
and authentically you.
Actually, the time is now
for you to learn this too.

Do whatever feels right
and follow your heart.
Being honest and sincere
is a major part.

Finally, own who you are,
and don't give in to trends.
You'll find your true self
instead of playing pretend.

Live by The Word

BEING BLESSED

(Read Matthew 5:3-12)

Scripture spotlight:

"Blessed are you when they revile and persecute you, and say all kinds of evil against you falsely for My sake."
– Matthew 5:11

L et us start with a question. Are we being true to ourselves or pretending to be people we are not? If it is the latter, what is the reason? While there can be many answers to this question, we must consider how we would speak, think, and act if we were being genuine.

Before we dig too deeply into our responses, we should know that God already accepts us for who we are. In Matthew 5:3-12, Jesus begins His initial sermon with what is popularly known as the Beatitudes. In this, Jesus tells the people listening that they are blessed regardless of who they are and their situation. And the beauty of this is that Jesus speaks about them precisely gaining what they need, even if it is on the opposite end of the spectrum in how they view themselves.

So, if Jesus could tell this to others, why would it not pertain to us? What goes without saying is that trials, tribulations, and inner conflict will increase when we are committed to staying true to God's Word and not the world's. We know this because Jesus says in verse 11 that people will revile, persecute, and say false and evil things against us for His sake. However, the beginning of the Scripture states that we will still be blessed.

Given this, what do we have to lose in being ourselves? What happens internally, externally, and eternally if people believe or say untruthful things about us? Our answers may vary, so Jesus tells us to rejoice and be glad due to our great reward in heaven (v. 12). Additionally, the same has happened to people before us. Therefore, let us be reassured based on not having to be the first or last in staying true to who God has called us to be.

Again, how would we speak, think, and act if we were our genuine selves? And since God already accepts us for who we are, are we ultimately asking if we accept ourselves for who we are?

RESTORE

It is better to be known for who you are than to change for just a few people.

_____

_____

_____

REFLECT

What will it take for me to accept God's view of me?

_____

_____

_____

RESPOND

Create and adhere to a list of non-negotiable items that commit you to be yourself.

_____

_____

_____

RECLAIM

Dear God, thank You for opening my eyes to genuineness. Please allow me to see myself the way You see me, as I do not want to conform to how the world sees me. In Jesus' name, Amen!

_____

_____

_____

CHAPTER 8:
HUMILITY

Definition:
Freedom from pride or arrogance.

ACCEPTANCE SPEECH

Wow.
Where do I start?
Not doing this before,
I guess I left my mark.

If I'm being honest,
I didn't do this alone.
I give thanks to my team
for these milestones.

All the other credit
is for those before.
I've been standing on their shoulders;
they allowed me to soar.

And God, more thanks;
it seems like time just flew.
I am who I am
because of You.

HUMBLED HINDSIGHT

(Read Matthew 3)

Scripture spotlight:
"And John tried to prevent Him, saying, 'I need to be baptized by You, and are You coming to me?'"
– Matthew 3:14

It is easy to believe our achievements, possessions, and relationships are solely related to our hard work and determination, so much so that we find ourselves saying, *I did this*, *I worked too hard for this*, or *I deserved this*. And no matter what *this* is, we often find ourselves taking most, if not all, credit for it.

But what have we truly obtained on our own? Jesus posed a similar question in Matthew 21:25 when He asked the chief priests and elders where John's (John the Baptist) baptism came from—heaven or men? They questioned their answers because of the reactions they would receive from Jesus and the people, but they settled on this response, "We do not know" (v. 27). Sometimes, we reply with uncertainty, too.

However, we know that John the Baptist had a calling over his life, or better yet, a role designated to him before he was born. Matthew 3:3 states, "For this is he who was spoken of by the prophet Isaiah, saying: The voice of one crying out in the wilderness: Prepare the way of the Lord." Isaiah lived many years before John the Baptist was even born. So, let us ask ourselves a critical question: what calling has God placed over our lives that we are reaping the benefits from now?

While John the Baptist was famous in many nations (Matthew 3:5) because of his ability to baptize people with water unto repentance, he knew there was someone greater than him to baptize with the Holy Spirit and fire (v. 11). He was also humble about it. He even said he was not worthy enough to carry that person's sandals (v. 11), and that person was Jesus.

John also admitted that Jesus should be baptizing him (v. 13). However, Jesus was humble enough to allow John to baptize Him (v. 15). If Jesus can do this and give credit to someone who was "unworthy," then how much more can we do for those who have paved the way for us? But most importantly, how much more can we do to honor and show God our appreciation for all He has done?

RESTORE

I have not done it by myself.

_____

_____

_____

REFLECT

How can I better acknowledge the outside factors that
positively impact my life?

_____

_____

_____

RESPOND

Contact multiple people to tell them how much they have
contributed to your success.

_____

_____

_____

RECLAIM

Lord, thank You for helping me realize what it took to be in my
position. Please continue to let me thank those individuals who
helped me along the way. In Jesus' name, Amen!

_____

_____

_____

CHAPTER 9:
IMPACT

Definition:
A significant or major effect.

THE STONE & THE STREAM

"I can make you change,"
the Stone informed the Stream.
"My thoughts and ways will move you
when I come onto the scene."

"Sure," the Stream replied.
"At first, you'll cause a ripple,
but when it's done and stationery
your influence is rather fickle.

Creating lasting change
is much more than you think.
Give to and build up others
without causing them to shrink.

Learn their wants and needs,
allow them to exceed
every expectation,
and your impact will succeed."

SUDDEN IMPACT

(Read John 6:1-14)

Scripture spotlight:

"There is a lad here who has five barley loaves and two small fish, but what are they among so many?"
– John 6:9

Having an impact on someone or something is one of the most extraordinary responsibilities we could ever have. However, what happens when we do not have enough influence in a challenging situation? Do we criticize ourselves, others, and possibly God? Do you need more confidence in this response? Do not worry because we are not the only ones who have had to answer this difficult question. John 6:1-14 explored this when the disciples encountered something very similar.

After Jesus had healed the sick of the "great multitude," He asked His disciple, Philip, where they could buy bread so everyone could eat (v. 5). While it was a test from Jesus, Philip immediately spoke about what they lacked instead of what they had (v. 6-7). Sound familiar? How often do we observe what Jesus has done for others and disregard what He has already done or can do for us?

It occurs more often than not if we are anything like the disciples. Even Andrew, another disciple, identified a young boy with five loaves of bread and two small fish and still questioned what those items would do for everyone (v. 9). However, notice who did not question it: the boy and Jesus.

Let us be reflective. The boy was willing to give all he had for Jesus and to meet the needs of others. Are we willing to do the same? Do we believe that Jesus can use what we have to impact the lives of others? If so, have we made ourselves available as the young boy did?

What is fascinating is that Jesus took what the boy offered, gave thanks, multiplied, and distributed it to bless everyone (v. 11). After everyone ate, there were twelve baskets filled with leftover fragments (v.13). With this, the true blessing occurred when those there started to believe in Jesus due to what they saw and experienced. Therefore, we should ask ourselves if we are allowing people to see Jesus for who and what He is by letting Him empower us in a way that is impactful to others.

RESTORE

The impact comes when we are willing to make sacrifices for others.

_____

_____

_____

REFLECT

What can I do differently to impact everyone I meet?

_____

_____

_____

RESPOND

Identify an area where you feel limited and use that to help someone else.

_____

_____

_____

RECLAIM

Lord, thank You for being the one who can use everything I have to improve the lives of others. Please do not let me take the opportunities You give me to do this for granted. In Jesus' name, Amen!

_____

_____

_____

CHAPTER 10:
JOY

Definition:
A source or cause of delight.

UNSPEAKABLE JOY

*I guess I'll try to tell you
how much Joy means to me.
My words won't do it justice,
but I'll try it with this plea.*

*Joy is instrumental
in everything we do.
Kind of like a guide in life,
Joy will get you through,*

*by eliminating worry,
eradicating stress,
diminishing anxiety,
and settling unrest.*

*I know I may be rambling
with everything I state,
but Joy should be a part of
everything you demonstrate.*

A JOYFUL JOURNEY

(Read Matthew 2:1-11)

Scripture spotlight:

"When they saw the star, they rejoiced with exceedingly great joy." – Matthew 2:10

We all know that joy exists, but for many of us, it has been elusive for years. This is not to say we have or will never experience it, but the journey mostly overshadows the destination when we do not give our full attention to the source of our joy. To observe another way to respond, let us explore the story of the wise men.

When we encounter them in Matthew 2:1-11, Jesus had been born in Bethlehem. Guided by a star in the East, the wise men arrived in Jerusalem looking for Jesus and found Herod instead. With this, we can relate to the wise men because it causes us to question the location of a promise we have heard of but have yet to witness.

Similar to what the wise men asked, we often ask ourselves, "Where is the thing that will bring us joy?" Yet, when the wise men asked the question, concern was not only from Herod but also from all of Jerusalem (v. 3). Herod asked the wise men where Christ was born. Interestingly enough, they said, "Bethlehem," due to what a prophet had written (v. 5).

So, why were the wise men even in Jerusalem? It could be to reflect on the promises given to them and spread the news of Jesus Christ, and if that is the case, we should ask ourselves how we can reflect on and share God's promises when located in a place where joy is absent. When searching for joy, we must not allow the *Herods* to fool us by supporting our pursuits with ulterior motives, which happens more often than not. In Herod's case, it occurred when he told the wise men to locate Jesus so he could worship Him too (v. 8).

Nevertheless, the wise men left, the star returned, and they were overwhelmed with joy when they saw it (v. 10); not because they had seen Jesus, but because they knew where to find Him. Given this, do we know where to find Jesus during our search for joy?

Lastly, once the wise men entered the house and saw the child Jesus with His mother, Mary, they worshiped Him (v. 11). They had physically seen and experienced joy. As a result, they gave Him gifts from their treasures, which leaves us asking, what are we willing to give to the journey, destination, and source of our joy when we ultimately find it?

RESTORE

The indescribable feeling of joy is only the beginning.

_____

_____

_____

REFLECT

How can I stay committed to being joyful when faced with
various uncertainties?

_____

_____

_____

RESPOND

Create, save, and revisit a list of everything that has brought
you joy.

_____

_____

_____

RECLAIM

Lord God, thank You for reminding me where the source of
my joy lies. Please help me stay in tune with this. In Jesus'
name, Amen!

_____

_____

_____

CHAPTER 11:
KNOWLEDGE

Definition:
The body of truth, information, and principles acquired by humankind.

THE GURU

"How do I acquire knowledge?"
the student gently asked.
"Do you know what it is you're seeking?"
the guru questioned fast.

"I'm seeking to be just like you.
Your knowledge reigns supreme."
The guru smiled and challenged back,
"Being you should be your dream.

You've placed me on a pedestal,
but we are both the same.
If you know exactly who you are,
there's nothing more to gain.

The knowledge that I have
is something that lies deep within.
The true quest is to know yourself,
so now, your journey begins."

WHO AM I?

(Read Matthew 16:13-20)

Scripture spotlight:
"He said to them, 'But who do you say that I am?'"
– Matthew 16:15

When we think about it, one question consistently comes up throughout our lifetimes. And if we have not gained the knowledge to answer it, how we respond to situations could be detrimental to our present and future selves. However, having the answer can establish a life trajectory we have never imagined. So what is the question? It is: who *am I*?

In Matthew 16:13-20, Jesus asked His disciples similar questions. The first one was, "Who do men say that I, the Son of Man, am" (v. 13)? The difference in His question is that He is not asking for Himself, as He's asking to see if people outside of His disciples can identify who He is. Do we not do the same thing? We may ask people close to us to express how others view us. However, let us think about this: how should the responses of people who do not know us affect what we know about ourselves?

If we observe Jesus, He moves on quickly when His disciples tell Him that people say He is one of the prophets, so much so that He does not even explore why people say it. He asks His next question, "But who do *you* say that I am" (v. 15)? This is insightful because His disciples should be able to answer this based on their experiences with Him.

Does this not sound like something we all want? It is difficult to comprehend, but sometimes, those closest to us do not see or defend who we think we are. The good news is that Peter saw Jesus' actual identity, "the Christ, the Son of the living God" (v. 16), due to God revealing it to him. After Peter's confession, Jesus gave him an affirmation: Simon Bar-Jonah, was the rock on which He would build His church (v. 17-18).

At that moment, Jesus identified who Peter was and what he would become. If Peter could receive this when he confessed, what would we gain if we did the same? While we weigh the outcomes of our responses, we must understand and accept the responsibilities that come with them.

Jesus gave clear instructions and expectations to His disciples when they revealed His identity. Therefore, we must be willing to know and follow His Word, which means our actions must display the image of Christ and His image for us. As a result, it ultimately changes the question of "*Who am I?*" to "*Who does God say I am?*"

RESTORE

God's image of you is much bigger than the image you have of yourself.

_____

_____

_____

REFLECT

What knowledge has Jesus given me to identify who He is and who I am?

_____

_____

_____

RESPOND

Speak with two friends to ask how they see you and determine if it aligns with God's image of you. If it does not, figure out how to change it.

_____

_____

_____

RECLAIM

Lord, thank You for allowing me to know You and myself. Please continue to help me see what You see in me. In Jesus' name, Amen!

_____

_____

_____

CHAPTER 12:
LOVE

Definition:
Unselfish, loyal, and benevolent concern for the good of another.

THE SEARCH FOR LOVE

I heard that Love was patient,
even kind, and endured all things.
To me, that sounded a little far-fetched,
but honestly, it had a nice ring.

However, Love was elusive
and much harder trying to find.
The years had started to all add up,
and I had only wasted time.

Then one day, it hit me.
My approach had to change.
I was doing way too much for Love,
and it wasn't doing the same.

That's when Love had found me.
It had been there all along.
I was blinded by the conditions,
but unconditionally, I belonged.

LOVE CHANGES THINGS

(Read John 3:16-21)

Scripture spotlight:

"For God so loved the world that He gave His only begotten Son, that whoever believes in Him should not perish but have everlasting life." – John 3:16

If we are anything alike, we can all remember the first time we thought we loved someone or something. Little did we know, we had no idea what the word meant. Now that we have lived a little bit longer and have far greater experiences, let us explore love in a much fuller context.

John 3:16 states, "For God so loved the world that He gave His only begotten Son, that whoever believes in Him should not perish but have everlasting life." Understanding this, we must ask, what would we give to the things we love? Would it be everything? Even if it requires us to relinquish another love of our lives? Deciding on this is something we need help with regularly. Yet, God makes it look so simple. But why? Could it be because God exemplifies something we have failed to master: selflessness? Or, in other words, love?

Let us think about it. God is so concerned with our needs and desires that He granted us eternal life through Jesus' sacrifice. Put differently, to shield us from condemnation for our words, thoughts, and actions, God surrendered a piece of God's self out of pure love. Therefore, if God is willing to do this for us, what will we do for God?

We often avoid that question and focus solely on what we are willing to do for ourselves, others, and our vices. And the same thing is shown in John 3:19-21 when it mentions people's love for the darkness over the light (because of the love for their "hidden" evil deeds). It also states that God is glorified when the acts of those who operate in the light are seen. This should make us question what is guiding our love. Is it darkness, light, or something else?

With answers in mind, can we reflect and honestly claim we are willing and ready to model the type of love God expects of us? Regardless of the answer, there has to be a way to become better stewards of God's love. Why? Because God did not give us Jesus for it to be any other way.

RESTORE

God's love is our salvation.

_____

_____

_____

REFLECT

How can people see the love of God through me?

_____

_____

_____

RESPOND

Get to know, accept, and love someone outside of the typical relationship you would build.

_____

_____

_____

RECLAIM

Lord, I want to thank You for the love You have shown to this world. Please allow me to do the same to bring glory to Your name. In Jesus' name, Amen!

_____

_____

_____

CHAPTER 13:
MOTIVATION

Definition:
A motivating force, stimulus, or influence.

<u>JUMPSTART</u>

*You try to turn it on
but can never get it going.
I'm here for assistance
and to get the juices flowing.*

*Leave your thoughts parked there
because this is an emergency.
Focus on the positive;
it's time for some urgency.*

*If there's negativity,
it shouldn't come from you.
Mishaps do happen;
use a spark to break through.*

*The next step is key:
get ready to ignite.
Take your foot off of the brake;
accelerate on-site.*

FOLLOW THE LEADER

(Read Matthew 4:18-22)

Scripture spotlight:
"They immediately left their nets and followed Him."
– Matthew 4:20

What is it that motivates us? Is it our firm beliefs on how things should go or our fight for self-preservation? Better yet, is it the concerns we have about the repercussions or rewards that follow our actions? Regardless of what it is, we must understand our "why" because the implications of our pursuits have a much more significant impact than ever imagined.

For example, let us examine the time Jesus selected His first disciples. While Peter and Andrew were fishing, Jesus said to them, "Follow Me, and I will make you fishers of men" (v. 19). After hearing that, Peter and Andrew immediately left their profession and followed Him. Knowing this, what does Jesus need to say to us to follow His calling over our lives?

Are we still thinking? If we got it now, what steered us from following that idea, urge, or conviction that was once a viable dream? Additionally, if we desire to be and do more, why do we not prioritize the opportunities we receive when they finally present themselves?

As the passage continues, Jesus does the same thing to another set of brothers named James and John. The difference in this story is that James and John were on a boat with their father when Jesus called them (v. 21). However, Jesus' words had the same impact. They left everything, including their father, to follow Him (v. 22). Therefore, are we motivated enough to depart from everything we know to follow Jesus through the unknown territories of our lives?

Before we submit an answer, notice that Jesus did not explain what it would take to accomplish what He had promised. He also did not expound upon the wins and losses they would experience. However, Jesus called them to do something they already had experience in, and more often than not, we find our successes in what we start when we lean on what we have previously learned. For that reason alone, what is Jesus calling us to do where we can utilize our honed skills?

Since we know the answers, we must remain confident in them to encounter the motivation that the initial disciples experienced. This is vital because our decision to move can change the course of history as theirs did in spreading the Gospel. Therefore, let us pay close attention to what guides us to follow God's call; it could be the one thing that separates us from others in motivating someone else to get closer to Jesus Christ.

RESTORE

Jesus is the only spark you need to follow the lead of your next calling.

_____

_____

_____

REFLECT

What is stopping me now, and how will I follow through on what is for me?

_____

_____

_____

RESPOND

Stop everything you are currently doing and start working on the next step to whatever God has called you to do.

_____

_____

_____

RECLAIM

Lord, thank You for motivating me to do what I have needed to do all along. Please guide me on this journey and give me whatever I need to make it through. In Jesus' name, Amen!

_____

_____

_____

CHAPTER 14:
NO

Definition:
An act or instance of refusing or denying by using the word "no."

NO-BILITY

The ability to say "no"
is beyond just a slogan.
It's a word of affirmation
that can always be spoken.

In any situation,
it creates independence.
Saying "no" by itself
is the complete sentence.

It'll carve out your character,
give you a peace of mind,
and allow you to be the narrator
of stories surpassing time.

So take it as a birth rite
or even a status change,
because knowing to say "no"
is something you can proclaim.

"KNOW" TEMPTATION

(Read Luke 4:1-13)

Scripture spotlight:

"And Jesus answered and said to him, "Get behind me, Satan! For it is written, 'You shall worship the Lord your God, and Him only you shall serve.'" – Luke 4:8

Saying "no" is hard. Especially when we say "no" to something that satisfies a perceived need. Truth be told, when that no becomes a yes, we often find ourselves with problems we cannot solve. Therefore, how do we remain steadfast in our no's? To answer this, let us examine what Jesus did when the devil tempted Him multiple times in Luke 4:1-13.

After Jesus fasted for forty days (v. 2), the devil tempted Him by saying, "If You are the Son of God, command this stone to become bread" (v. 3). And while this targeted Jesus' physiological needs, His response (v. 4) allows us to see how He entrusted His life to the Word of God. Understanding this, let us ask, where do we put our trust? And, what would we be able to accomplish if we craved God's Word as much as we did other things?

While we grapple with our responses, the text shows that the second temptation involved the psychological need for prestige. The devil showed Jesus all the kingdoms of the world and promised authority over them if He worshiped the devil (v. 5-6). However, Jesus' rebuttal committed His worship and service to God alone, making us ask ourselves: what are we worshiping? God, or other things?

The third temptation occurred when the devil took Jesus to the top of the temple and told Him to throw Himself down (v. 9). Again, the devil uses the statement, "If you are the Son of God" (v. 9), and tells Him that the angels will protect Him if He is. Let us think. Have we ever had someone dictate how things would go for us based on particular actions? Additionally, how often was the outcome tied to how people perceived us rather than how we saw ourselves?

Gratefully, Jesus knew who He was and stated, "It has been said, 'You shall not tempt the Lord your God'" (v. 12). Yet, we constantly tempt God each day by pursuing things outside God's will—in turn, causing us to request protection and forgiveness from our consistent wrongdoings. Regardless, how do we receive support?

Notice what happened when Jesus continuously said "no." The devil stopped (v. 13), and Matthew 4:11 noted that "angels came and ministered to Him." If we repeatedly say "no," we will receive the same thing. However, the devil is always looking for an "opportune time" to return and guide us down a path of destruction (Luke 4:13). Therefore, let us be on guard and follow Jesus' example. We may never know if we are the example others look to during their struggles.

RESTORE

Know when and how to say "no."

_____

_____

_____

REFLECT

What holds me back from saying "no," and how will I move
past it when the time comes?

_____

_____

_____

RESPOND

Say "no" to at least five things that will hinder you.

_____

_____

_____

RECLAIM

God, thank You for Your saving grace and mercy when
temptation comes. Please build my capacity and willingness to
say "no" more times than not. In Jesus' name, Amen!

_____

_____

_____

CHAPTER 15:
OPTIMISM

Definition:
An inclination to put the most favorable construction upon actions and events or to anticipate the best possible outcome.

THE GLASS

"What do you see, Glass?"
someone asked of me.
I responded, "Hmm, I see
a lot of possibilities.

Sure, I can complain,
but I can't focus on opinions.
Whether half-full or empty,
I ultimately have dominion.

I can carry different things,
display any reflection,
adjust for different optics,
and also provide protection.

But that's just a sample
and not the full list.
So don't put me into a box;
my purpose is limitless."

PRESUME THE POSITIVE

(Read Mark 10:17-31)

Scripture spotlight:

"But Jesus looked at them and said, "With men it is impossible, but not with God; for with God all things are possible." – Mark 10:27

I t is tough to stay positive when negative situations create unfortunate setbacks. Additionally, optimism often dwindles when God creates opportunities to face our fears. Given this, how do we persist when our expectations are unmet? The story of the rich man in Mark 10:17-27 answers this question and highlights who we are amid adversity. While there may be differences between the rich man and us, the one thing we have in common is the desire to receive something from Jesus.

The rich man wanted to know what he could do to inherit eternal life (v. 17). Our thoughts are similar as we crave to understand what it takes to achieve something. However, will we be satisfied with Jesus' response? The rich man was unsatisfied with what Jesus had said and expressed his "self-proclaimed" accomplishments to Him (v. 20). Jesus immediately identified his deficiency by telling him what he lacked (v. 21). Let us reflect. How often have we told God what we have done without giving God the glory?

When the rich man heard this, he was sad and left sorrowful because he placed his trust in his possessions instead of what he could have possessed with Jesus (v. 22). If this was us, how would our perspectives need to shift to trust God's ability more so than our own?

Jesus explored this in a conversation with His disciples. He discussed how difficult it was for rich people to enter the kingdom of God (v. 23). His disciples were shocked and questioned, "Who then can be saved" (v. 26)? Jesus then stated, "With men it is impossible, but not with God; for with God all things are possible" (v. 27). Therefore, if all things are possible with God, even something as grand as eternal life, why would we not remain optimistic that God can work everything out in our favor?

RESTORE

There is always a positive to counteract a negative.

_____

_____

_____

REFLECT

How will I remain optimistic in unexpected situations that negatively impact my life?

_____

_____

_____

RESPOND

Look for and share the positive aspects of any adverse situation or outlook that comes your way.

_____

_____

_____

RECLAIM

Lord, thank You for showing me who You are and the power behind your endless capabilities. Please continue strengthening my trust in You so I can remain optimistic and appreciative throughout whatever I go through. In Jesus' name, Amen!

_____

_____

_____

CHAPTER 16:
PERSEVERANCE

Definition:
Continued effort to do or achieve something despite difficulties, failure, or opposition.

FIT FOR THE FIGHT

This isn't something new;
read the tale of the tape.
I've been prepared by my training,
so just study my pace.

I'll even go toe-to-toe
and do whatever it takes.
When I get hit, I'll probably bend,
but I will never break.

If I'm down on the ground,
then don't count me out.
The eight seconds are enough
to stand and finish the bout.

But when that final bell rings
yes, the judging commenced,
I'll raise my hand as the victor,
since my will didn't flinch.

PRESS ON

(Read Matthew 24:3-14)

Scripture spotlight:
"But he who endures to the end shall be saved."
– Matthew 24:13

Wat do we do when times are rough? Are the moments warranted where we ask God, "Why me?" How do we respond when God says "No," or "Not yet?" These are difficult questions with complex answers, but the desire to survive and thrive is at the core of each one.

In Matthew 24:3-14, Jesus answers His disciples' questions but more explicitly responds to one around the identification of the end times and His return. If we are being candid, there have been times when we have asked Jesus a similar question. The question might look like this: when will you show up and take this suffering, pain, or whatever I am going through away?

What is beautiful about this exchange between Jesus and His disciples is that Jesus gives them an answer, which He also does for us. He tells them not to be deceived by people claiming to be Him or concerned about rumors of wars and other troubling signs (v. 5-12). Let us be honest. When did we last trust others, rumors, or signs over God?

Do not worry. It happens, and Jesus stated that this is only the "beginning of sorrows" (v. 8). He then mentions that "they" will deliver, kill, and hate us for His name's sake (v. 9). Continuing, He described how love would cease, and chaos would ensue (v. 10-11). Likewise, this is what happens when we lose sight of God in all the circumstances we face.

However, we can find encouragement in knowing that the people "who endure to the end shall be saved" (v. 13). Hence, don't avoid it. Experience adversity, respond to it, and stand firm in knowing God will ultimately deliver and bless us according to His will.

Additionally, we have a duty to respond in the future. Jesus says the end will come when the Gospel is "preached in all the world" (v. 14). Therefore, let us ask, how will we recognize the blessing in our struggles and be a witness in spreading the Gospel of Jesus Christ?

RESTORE

The fight continues as long as you do!

_____

_____

_____

REFLECT

What challenges have I recently faced, and how did I give God
the glory in everything I went through?

_____

_____

_____

RESPOND

Engage with someone experiencing hardships and allow God
to use your story as a testimony.

_____

_____

_____

RECLAIM

God, thank You for allowing me to grow from the challenges I
have faced. Please continue to give me the strength I need to
continue and the ability to encourage others by sharing what
You have done for me. In Jesus' name, Amen!

_____

_____

_____

CHAPTER 17:
QUESTION

Definition:
An act or instance of asking.

21 QUESTIONS

What are you afraid to answer?
Is it something you need to find?
What? Is it buried deep within?
Is uncovering it worth your time?

Is there someone that can help you?
What will they really demand?
Would they understand their role? For you?
Are you willing to stick to the plan?

Can you ask yourself these questions?
When? Did you think it wouldn't be now?
How? Isn't that up to you to decide?
If not, what will you allow?

Do you honestly feel prepared for this?
Is there much more you can do?
Yes? Isn't it time for you to start?
Will it make you feel anew?

LESSON LEARNED

(Read John 8:1-12)

Scripture spotlight:

"When Jesus had raised Himself up and saw no one but the woman, He said to her, "Woman, where are those accusers of yours? Has no one condemned you?"
– John 8:10

We often ask questions because we are trying to understand the presented information. However, there are moments when our questions are disingenuous and designed to belittle, demonize, or manipulate the messenger. The difference between the two can be minuscule, so how do we stay committed to asking questions that will benefit ourselves and the lives of others?

When we interact with the text of John 8:1-12, we can begin posing questions. Why was a woman caught in adultery brought to Jesus when He was teaching in the temple (v. 3)? What were the scribes and Pharisees doing when they found the woman? Lastly, why did they not bring the other person who participated in adultery with her?

These are all great questions worth asking; there could be more, but we know why they did this. It was to test and accuse Jesus of something, as they wanted to compare His teachings to the law of Moses. If this was their reasoning, then we should reflect on the motives behind our questions to God.

Jesus ignored their questioning by bending down and writing on the ground with His finger (v. 6). Being reflective, does Jesus do the same to our questions when they are not pure?

Maybe, maybe not, but as they continued to ask, just like us, Jesus responded by saying, "He who is without sin among you, let him throw a stone at her first" (v. 7).

Jesus resumed writing on the ground, and the people were confronted with a question: am I in a position to cast judgment on an individual when I'm just as sinful? While the question is great for them, we can also ask it ourselves. And once we do, will our responses be the same?

After everyone left, Jesus asked the woman two questions. They were, "Where are your accusers" and, "...has no one condemned you" (v. 10)? The woman said "No one," and Jesus responded, "Neither do I" (v. 11). Notice Jesus did not condemn but questioned to show the woman who He was and His love for her. Therefore, we should ask ourselves, what do our questions say about us?

RESTORE

Ask the "right" questions.

REFLECT

How can I change my questions rooted in condemnation to
ones covered in a culture of concern and care?

RESPOND

For the next twenty-four hours, only ask questions for the care
and betterment of others.

RECLAIM

Lord, help me to ask questions that benefit the lives of others.
Please allow me to discern what is good versus evil, and give me
the courage to question those trying to harm. In Jesus' name,
Amen!

CHAPTER 18:
RELATIONSHIP

Definition:
A state of affairs existing between those having relations or dealings.

THE FORTUNE TELLER

"So, you want to know your future?"
the fortune teller asked.
Then continued, "Well, it's simple.
Start by moving from the past.

Another thing that's vital
and will pay dividends:
the future that you want
will be influenced by your friends.

The bonds you choose are crucial,
as they'll help or stunt your growth.
Stay away from liabilities;
assets assist the most.

So, examine your relationships
to see which ones should stay.
Your goals will drive your strategy
and won't lead you astray."

Live by The Word

CONNECTED

(Read John 15:1-8)

Scripture spotlight:

"I am the vine, you are the branches. He who abides in Me, and I in him, bears much fruit; for without Me you can do nothing." – John 15:5

As we know, we cannot do anything in this world without having relationships. While our minds may only consider romantic ones, we should also acknowledge our platonic and familial relationships. And whether our relationships have helped or hindered us, we must remember that we are the product of whatever connects us.

Jesus speaks to this in John 15:1-8 when He described Himself as the vine and God as the vinedresser. He then stated that He would remove every branch connected to Him that does not produce fruit, and the branches that do produce will be pruned to produce more (v. 2). This may lead us to question how our previous or current relationships have followed this model.

While our answers may differ in certain aspects, we can all agree that our impact on others is a huge responsibility. Therefore, if we are considered the vines, who would our branches be, and what would they produce? Also, notice that Jesus says we are clean because of His spoken Word (v. 3). Since this is the case, what can others say about themselves based on the words we speak to them?

Now, let us make one thing clear: we are not, nor will we ever be, Jesus. As He shares, "without [Him] [we] can do nothing" (v. 5), which means people can do a lot of things without us, but they need to be connected to Him to do everything. Given this, what are we doing to contribute to people's positive connection to Christ?

Jesus explains what would happen to individuals who are disconnected or connected. Those who are disconnected will be cast aside, thrown into the fire, and burned, while the connected will have His words, ask for their desires, and have them done for them (v. 6-7). As we think about that, what are we doing to stay connected to Jesus?

While we contemplate our relationships, we should also recognize that our relationships with each other and Jesus are not solely for our betterment. Ultimately, God gets the glory through our blessings (v. 8). Therefore, our relationships should outwardly display God's love, allowing us to build a deeper connection with Jesus Christ.

RESTORE

With God, we can do all things.

_____

_____

_____

REFLECT

How would my relationships shift if I connected more with
God?

_____

_____

_____

RESPOND

Converse with someone about how your relationship with
Christ impacts your relationship with them.

_____

_____

_____

RECLAIM

Lord God, thank You for all the relationships I have had in my
lifetime. Please continue to use me to spread Your love and
allow me to see You when I have trouble seeing the good in
others. In Jesus' name, Amen!

_____

_____

_____

CHAPTER 19:
SUPPORT

Definition:
Assist, help.

GOOD COUNSEL

I shall help you with it all
when it seems like you're in trouble.
I can place some things in motion,
so there'll be no need to struggle.

I will issue you this gift
without you having much to bear.
There is a need to carry you;
your burdens can be shared.

The mental piece is tough,
and it's something we'll get through.
The witness needs a little work;
your testimony, too.

And when you stand before the judge,
I'll be right by your side.
It'll be a lot to comprehend
the things you'll feel inside.

SUPPORTING THE MISSION
(Read Luke 10:25-37)
Scripture spotlight:
"So which of these three do you think was neighbor to him who fell among the thieves?" – Luke 10:36

For many of us, offering support is extremely difficult, especially when the need arises for an individual we do not know or someone we have previously helped. However, finding ways to aid others, despite limited resources, becomes more manageable once we realize the importance of our actions.

In Luke 10:25-37, a lawyer tested Jesus by asking Him how to inherit eternal life. Jesus responded by asking him, "What is written in the law? What is your reading of it" (v. 26)? Is it not interesting that Jesus asked the lawyer to interpret the law? Given this, why do we ask God questions we already have answers to based on our lived experiences?

The lawyer answered correctly by saying, "Love God" and love "your neighbor as yourself" (v. 27). Afterwards, he asked Jesus another question: "Who is my neighbor" (v.29)? In response, Jesus shared a story about a man who received support from a Samaritan after a priest and Levite had passed him by (v. 30-35). Knowing this, how would we respond if we saw someone in need? Before we answer, let us reflect on a common situation. What do we usually do when we see an individual on the side of the road asking for help? Could our inaction in those situations be similar to why the priest and Levite did not help the man?

If so, let us note how the lawyer answered his question after Jesus' story. The lawyer said the neighbor to the man was the one "who showed mercy" (v. 37). Because of this, Jesus expects us to support others, as He said, "Go and do likewise" (v. 37), to the lawyer's response, which means we must be willing to aid our neighbors.

Additionally, we must recognize that the Samaritan was an unlikely source of support for the man due to the conflict between their nations. So, let us acknowledge that we may not be the first option for help, but God uses us, just like the Samaritan, to display God's character and true mercies.

RESTORE

You can support others because others have supported you.

_____

_____

_____

REFLECT

What can I do differently to allow God to use me to
demonstrate His mercy?

_____

_____

_____

RESPOND

Find a way to support at least three different people today.

_____

_____

_____

RECLAIM

Lord, thank You for the ability to support someone else
because you have supported me. Please continue to use my
giving in the way You see fit. In Jesus' name, Amen!

_____

_____

_____

CHAPTER 20:
TRUTH

Definition:
Sincerity in action, character, and utterance.

MORAL COMPASS

I followed the path I'd seen,
even though it wasn't for me.
Every step I took seemed broken,
but I continued for false guarantees.

I cross-referenced every location
because I had lost my way.
I was allured by the grandeur of greed,
all of the lying took things away.

When I realized the wrongs I had done,
I decided to take a new course.
What happened was short of amazing.
I was able to cite a new source.

The lessons I learned were priceless.
I'm sure they'll never depart.
My quest started right where it'd finished
because the truth was there in my heart.

VERIFIED

(Read John 18:33-40)

Scripture spotlight:

"Pilate said to Him, "What is truth?" And when he had said this, he went out again to the Jews, and said to them, "I find no fault in Him at all." – John 18:38

How do we know what is true? Disinformation is often shared so others can profit from our positions based on a collective belief. Therefore, it is essential to think and respond critically before simply accepting the ideas and opinions of others. Pilate did this in John 18:33-40 when he conversed with Jesus. Instead of taking the chief priests' word for Jesus' "wrongdoing," Pilate went to the source to obtain information (v. 33).

How often do we miss this step in determining what is true? Additionally, how often do we fail to gain the perspectives of others involved? Pilate asked Jesus if He was the "King of the Jews" (v. 33). Jesus responded by asking Pilate if he was asking for himself or others (v. 34). Pilate then tried to determine what Jesus had done without considering Jesus' character (v. 35), which is often similar to what we do. Understanding this, what makes us care more about a few actions of a person, as opposed to the whole character of that same individual?"

Afterward, Jesus explained His kingdom and what would have happened if it was of this world (v. 36). Immediately, Pilate asked Jesus about being a king again. However, this time, Pilate asked to understand Jesus for himself (v. 37), which should have us ask, what causes this shift of personal understanding instead of solely relying on group beliefs?

Another question is, how do we know what is true even if we have received it from the source? This is the same question Pilate asked when Jesus told him that everyone who hears His voice is of the truth (v. 37). Pilate phrased his question by asking, "What is truth?" before he found no fault in Jesus (v. 38).

It is interesting how we can identify the truth as well. We can sense when something feels off or if a story or situation is rooted in a limited portion of fact but covertly wrapped in falsehoods. But to consistently identify the truth, let us follow Jesus' blueprint of "hearing His voice" and continuously ask, are we listening to the right things?

RESTORE

The truth is the guiding light for all that we do and encounter.

_____

_____

_____

REFLECT

How can I get better at discerning God's voice in every situation?

_____

_____

_____

RESPOND

Pick one big idea you believe in that others may not. Analyze and question why you believe in it and see what God says.

_____

_____

_____

RECLAIM

Lord God, thank You for providing me with a sound mind. Please allow me to be responsible and committed to the thoughts and ideas that come from You. In Jesus' name, Amen!

_____

_____

_____

CHAPTER 21:
URGENCY

Definition:
A force or impulse that impels or constrains.

THE SENSE OF URGENCY

Do you notice what is happening?
I'm not sure you do.
Time is of the essence,
and I hope you hear this too.

It's really now or never,
so get up, go, and grab it.
If not, you'll miss your moment;
life moves quicker than imagined.

The chance is right in front of you,
so close that you can taste it.
Tomorrow is not promised,
and today cannot be wasted.

If you manage it correctly,
then you'll smell the sweet success.
Your world can change just like that,
so only bring your best.

STAY READY

(Read Matthew 24:36-44)

Scripture spotlight:

"Watch therefore, for you do not know what hour your Lord is coming." – Matthew 24:42

Consider this: time is the only thing we equally have. While we may not have the same number of years, we have the same twenty-four hours each day. But how would we respond if we truly reflected on the limitations of our time? Jesus referenced this in Matthew 24:36-44, when He continued His conversation around the unknown day and hour of the end times. He mentioned how it would mirror the days of Noah and highlighted how unprepared everyone was when the flood came (v. 37-39). Remember, Noah was able to prepare because he found grace in God's eyes (Genesis 6:8).

Therefore, what can we do differently to follow God's plans better? Keep in mind, Noah built an ark to God's specifications (Genesis 6:14-16), and people may have wondered what he was doing. This leads us to ask, what has God requested us to do that may seem excessive to others? Additionally, are we spending our time appropriately to ensure it gets done?

Returning to the passage, Jesus mentioned how some people would be taken, and others left behind (Matthew 24:40-41). He encouraged everyone to watch and be ready for the moment. Thus, would we be prepared if the moment was tomorrow? If not, what would we have to do to change that?

Additionally, Jesus alluded to this question when He gave the example of the master of the house. Jesus stated that the master would protect his home from a thief if he knew when the thief was coming (v. 43). Again, we do not get that luxury, so how will we utilize our time to be and stay ready?

Since Jesus told us to be ready due to not knowing His return, the previous question asked becomes even more critical. However, once we answer that question, another question arises: how do we help others get ready once we are ready ourselves?

RESTORE

Urgency requires more than a mindset. It also requires action.

_____

_____

_____

REFLECT

What will it truly take for me to be ready for the moment?

_____

_____

_____

RESPOND

Find out what is holding someone else back from being ready
and assist them in staying prepared.

_____

_____

_____

RECLAIM

Lord, thank You for moving me in the direction I need to go.
Please give me a spirit of readiness and the ability to respond.
In Jesus' name, Amen!

_____

_____

_____

CHAPTER 22:
VISION

Definition:
Unusual discernment or foresight.

GETTING FOCUSED

"We're trying to improve our vision.
It's very hard to see."
We sighed, "We need assistance
and corrective clarity.

The lenses we've been using
haven't brought things into focus.
Our contacts weren't working,
and the outlook just seemed hopeless."

"Let's see what's going on.
Can y'all spell this out for me?"
The expert had some questions
and needed our history.

We eventually found the problem.
Our vision was misaligned.
We had to follow a plan,
which improved it all over time.

SIGHTSEEING

(Read Luke 18:35-43)

Scripture spotlight:

"Saying, 'What do you want Me to do for you?'
He said, 'Lord, that I may receive my sight.'"
– Luke 18:41

There has always been that one vision we have constantly tried to obtain. However, let us recognize that our narrow perspectives may limit our desperately sought-after visions. Therefore, we must find ways to enhance them by asking God to assist us in seeing all the possibilities. This is apparent in the story of the blind man begging on the side of the road in Luke 18:35-44. Once he heard from the crowd that Jesus was walking by, he called out to Him, asked for mercy, and awaited His response.

Considering this, how often have we cried out to Jesus for help when others were around? After the blind man initially called out, people from the crowd told him to be quiet (v. 39). If this happened to him, it could also happen to us. Therefore, how many times have we let the opinions of others impact our paths toward gaining our visions? Additionally, how do we move beyond self-doubt when things do not go according to how we have planned them?

If we follow the blind man's response, we should continue calling out to Jesus regardless of our circumstances. When Jesus' attention went to the blind man, He "commanded" that the blind man be brought to Him (v. 40). Let us reflect: when was the last time Jesus used others to bring us closer to Him so that we could be one step closer to actualizing our visions?

Jesus asked the blind man what he wanted to be done for him, and the blind man asked for his sight (v. 41). The beauty in this is that the blind man already had everything he needed to secure it. While his vision was limited, he used what he had to get what he wanted. Knowing this, what aspects of our lives have we overlooked that can aid us in our vision pursuits?

When Jesus gave the blind man his sight, Jesus stated that it was due to his faith (v. 42). This should make us ask, what stops us from attaining the visions we want? While we reflect on this, let us acknowledge that the blind man praised and followed God after he received his sight, which caused others to praise God, too (v. 43). Given this, the actual question is, why does God allow us to have the visions we want when it aligns with God's will?

RESTORE

Visions demand a commitment to see what God sees in us.

_____

_____

_____

REFLECT

How can I ensure God gets the credit for every aspect of my vision?

_____

_____

_____

RESPOND

Create a vision and six actionable steps you can take to attain it.

_____

_____

_____

RECLAIM

Lord, thank You for opening my eyes to see that I have everything I need to accomplish my vision. Please grant me the opportunity to acknowledge You throughout the process. In Jesus' name, Amen!

_____

_____

_____

CHAPTER 23:
WISDOM

Definition:
Abilities to discern inner qualities and relationships.

SAGE

I want to plant this seed,
and I hope it will take root.
The location isn't perfect,
but that detail is minute.

I say this with full knowledge
and experience as well.
It really makes a difference
when the seed breaks from its shell.

But in order to see growth,
you must first know how to sow.
Allow the light to shine
and watch what rises from below.

The nourishment is crucial;
keep an eye on how it's fed,
and when the harvest comes,
make sure it's something that can spread.

THE FOUNDATION

(Read Matthew 7:24-29)

Scripture spotlight:

"Therefore whoever hears these sayings of Mine, and does them, I will liken him to a wise man who built his house on the rock:" – Matthew 7:24

Acquiring and applying wisdom may be more complex than we once believed. While wisdom combines information, knowledge, and experience to make appropriate decisions, sometimes opportunities to capture, display, and provide it become highly fleeting. Nevertheless, we should continue to maximize the moments we have to share or demonstrate our wisdom with the ones we encounter.

In Matthew 7:24-29, Jesus shared information with those He taught around His sayings. He equated people who listened to and acted upon His words to a "wise man who built his house on the rock" (v. 24). Jesus also described how the elements were no match for the house due to its solid foundation (v. 25). Therefore, are we wise enough to listen to Jesus?

Before we answer that, let us think about what Jesus has asked us to do over our lifetimes. After careful contemplation, have we been obedient to God's Word in every aspect of our lives? If not, why do we consistently sabotage ourselves when we have the wisdom to follow God's directions? While the answers may range in scope, each can be rooted in self-sufficiency.

Due to this, Jesus continued His lesson on house building when He discussed those who heard His sayings but did not respond accordingly. He compared those individuals to "a foolish man who built his house on the sand" (v. 26). Again, Jesus explored what happened to the house when attacked by the elements; in this instance, the house could not withstand them and ultimately experienced a great fall (v. 27).

Consider how great our falls have been when we did not follow the wisdom God gave us through ourselves or others. Additionally, what testimonies do we have of God sustaining us through life's storms simply because we were wise enough to follow God's Word? Regardless of our answers, we should see the differences in our experiences based on the wisdom we obtained from each situation.

The exciting part is that the people listening to Jesus felt the same way (v. 28). They were amazed because He taught with authority and not like the scribes (v. 29). Therefore, how do we share wisdom learned from Jesus with others who may not know who He is?

RESTORE

Wisdom is gained through learning, responding, and discerning life experiences.

_____

_____

_____

REFLECT

What can I do when I find myself not listening to the wisdom of others?

_____

_____

_____

RESPOND

Think about something you have learned during your life's journey and share it with someone who may be on the path of making a similar discovery.

_____

_____

_____

RECLAIM

Thank You, God, for giving me the wisdom I need to follow You. Please continue to teach me what I need so I can share it with others who may need the same thing. In Jesus' name, Amen!

_____

_____

_____

CHAPTER 24:
X-FACTOR

Definition:
A circumstance, quality, or person that has a strong but unpredictable influence.

LIGHTS, CAMERA, ACTION

You have "it!"
It's something you can't disguise.
I see it in all your actions;
no need to act surprised.

Some say that it's a gift
and ascribe it to your birth.
There's more than just having it;
living it takes work.

So practice it every day.
Learn as much as you can.
Make necessary adjustments.
Determine where to expand.

Regardless, bring your best.
Don't worry about any stress.
Remember, you are the person
you need to impress.

THAT'S THE SPIRIT

(Read John 14:1-6)

Scripture spotlight:

"Jesus said to him, "I am the way, the truth, and the life.
No one comes to the Father except through Me."
– John 14:6

How often have we viewed others as having access to something we did not? Better yet, how many times have we thought other individuals were better off than us? If this has been our thinking, we may have constantly dismissed the power that guides and lies within us.

Let us consider the conversation Jesus had with His disciples in John 14:1-6. In short, He told them not to be worried because they believed in God (v. 1). And since they believed in God, they could also believe in Him (v. 1). Therefore, if we can believe in God, then why do we doubt what Jesus has given us?

As Jesus continued His conversation, He spoke of future promises by stating that He would "prepare a place for them" and return to retrieve them (v. 2-3). If Jesus is willing to do this for His disciples, what makes us think He is not willing to do it for us? Given this, what do we feel we lack to trust God fully?

If we are being honest, we all have that one thing. However, Thomas was the first to admit it when Jesus told them they knew how to get to where He was going (v. 4). Thomas questioned Jesus' statement and asked, how could they know the way if they did not know the destination (v. 5)? Does this sound like us? If so, how many times have we lost sight of Jesus due to not knowing the place He was leading us?

When Jesus responded to Thomas, He told him that He is the way, truth, and life, and that the only way to God is through Him (v. 6). As a result, He gave Thomas information on how to get to where he *should* be going, which raises another important question: are we going after everything *we* want or what *God* wants?

While we ponder this, consider that we all have a choice in determining our futures. Regardless of the directions we take, we must fully understand that our journeys look different depending on our decisions to follow Jesus. Ultimately, He is our X-factor and allows us to see God through everything we encounter and experience.

RESTORE

Jesus is all you need to get to where you are going.

_____

_____

_____

REFLECT

How might I better follow the path that Jesus has given to me?

_____

_____

_____

RESPOND

Find someone in a position you want to be in and figure out how that person got there.

_____

_____

_____

RECLAIM

Lord, thank You for allowing me to see that You can change everything. Please give me the strength to stay committed to where You lead me. In Jesus' name, Amen!

_____

_____

_____

CHAPTER 25:
YOUTHFULNESS

Definition:
Having the vitality, behavior, or appearance of youth.

BORN AGAIN

*You don't have to be young
to truly make a difference.
Just believe in your heart
that everybody has deliverance.*

*It starts with an idea
and a willingness to try.
Fearlessness when uncertainty
appears as a lie.*

*Up next is the passion
that aligns with the purpose.
Add vigor and rigor,
and youthfulness will resurface.*

*This helps all encountered
feel that they are free,
empowered to succeed,
and the peace to just be.*

FOREVER YOUNG

(Read Matthew 18:1-5)

Scripture spotlight:

"...and said, "Assuredly, I say to you, unless you are converted and become as little children, you will by no means enter the kingdom of heaven."
– Matthew 18:3

What would we give for a do-over? Not necessarily one that would have minimum impact, but one that would change the trajectory of our lives. Would our responses shift from the initial ones, or would we go through the situations again to futuristically lean on what we learned from that moment?

Matthew 18:1-5 tells of a moment when Jesus' disciples asked Him, "Who then is the greatest in the kingdom of heaven" (v. 1)? While we can view this question from multiple perspectives, we can all reflect on the many times we wanted acknowledgment as the best in something. However, according to Jesus, we should consider something else.

In response to His disciples' question, Jesus called for a child and told them they would not enter the kingdom of heaven unless they were "converted and became as little children" (v. 3). But why would Jesus say this? Is it because little children depend more on their providers than on their own merits? If true, what do we rely on to define our greatness?

Jesus continued by telling His disciples that the greatest in the kingdom of heaven are the ones who humble themselves as children (v. 4). But again, what is Jesus teaching us through the example of little children? Could He want us to mirror their youthfulness, including their passion and excitement for learning and doing new things? If so, what is stopping us from doing that?

Another thing Jesus mentioned was that whoever received a child in His name received Him (v. 5). What is interesting about this is how little children receive each other. They have no judgment and accept one another just as they are. And this is how Jesus accepts us and expects us to do the same. However, can we say that we do this for everyone we meet? If not, why is that?

While Jesus' answer may not have been what the disciples expected, it opened their minds and possibly eliminated the selfishness in their original question. In turn, it allowed us to see the characteristics of children we needed to resemble to do the will and work of God. Now that we know this, will we wish to start over or use this information to adjust what we currently do?

RESTORE

You do not have to be young to display youthful qualities.

_____

_____

_____

REFLECT

What do I have to do differently to exhibit a youthful persona?

_____

_____

_____

RESPOND

Determine a positive character trait of a child you would like to strengthen in yourself and practice it for the next twenty-four hours.

_____

_____

_____

RECLAIM

God, I am grateful that You gave me the blueprint for entering Your kingdom. Please give me the courage and skill to acquire the traits needed to please You. In Jesus' name, Amen!

_____

_____

_____

CHAPTER 26:
ZEAL

Definition:
Eagerness and ardent interest in pursuit of something.

ARE YOU ZEALOUS?

What do you have to envy
when you're eager for your pursuits?
Your enthusiasm is different,
so comparisons are moot.

Continue to chase your dreams
and go after everything you've wanted.
If not, you might regret it
and may ultimately feel haunted.

But don't let those desires
consume every aspect of your life.
Your heart, mind, and soul
are worth much more than what's in sight.

And once you do achieve,
make sure it's something you maintain.
The example that you set
can help other people with their gains.

Live by The Word

DETERMINED DESIRES

(Read Mark 16:14-20)

Scripture spotlight:
*"And they went out and preached everywhere,
the Lord working with them and confirming the Word
through the accompanying signs. Amen."*
– Mark 16:20

We are all gifted with the desires God has placed on our hearts and the abilities to achieve them. However, many of us will continuously capture the things we are chasing, while others may never experience them. Why is that? What is prohibiting us from living what God has called us to do?

In Mark 16:14-20, Jesus rebuked His disciples for their disbelief. After being with Him for years and knowing of the resurrection, His disciples did not believe it when others saw Him first (v. 14). Sound familiar? How often have we discredited someone else's testimony because we did not see or experience it? While we think about this, we must consider that the disciples still received what they longed for: an opportunity to see the resurrected Jesus.

Additionally, we should note that Jesus did not dwell on the rebuke. He immediately assigned them the task of preaching the Gospel to every creature in the world (v. 15). Therefore, let us ask: what assignment has Jesus given us after He needed to correct our behaviors or actions? What promises has He made to give us a future outlook on carrying out the task? Jesus told His disciples that those who believed, would be saved, and those who did not, would be condemned (v. 16). Let us assume that their experience with Jesus gave them what they needed to consider the task and recognize what was achievable.

After Jesus finished speaking to the disciples, He went to heaven and sat with God (v. 19). Then, the disciples went out and followed the assignment Jesus gave them by preaching the Gospel throughout the entire world (v. 20). Jesus was with them while they did this and displayed the things He said would happen for them (v. 20).

Understand that God sees us all as disciples. Therefore, we should consider the question: what would we be able to accomplish if we wholeheartedly believed in and relentlessly followed what Jesus told us to do? Likewise, what would others gain from what we passionately pursued? Once we know those answers, we only need to focus strictly on the path God has perfectly prepared for us.

RESTORE

God will always give you the desires of your heart if they align with God's will.

_____

_____

_____

REFLECT

How will I improve my commitment and interest in what God has for me?

_____

_____

_____

RESPOND

Identify what God has called you to do, and dedicate yourself to experiencing everything that comes with it.

_____

_____

_____

RECLAIM

Lord, I am Yours. Please use me and help me see how You have made me commit my spirit to do everything You would have me do. In Jesus' name, Amen!

_____

_____

_____

MY WORDS

A: _____

B: _____

C: _____

D: _____

E: _____

F: _____

G: _____

H: _____

I: _____

J: _____

Live by The Word

K: _____

L: _____

M: _____

N: _____

O: _____

P: _____

Q: _____

R: _____

S: _____

T: _____

U: _____

V: _____

W: _____

X: _____

Y: _____

Z: _____

ACKNOWLEDGEMENTS

My heart is full, and I am grateful for everything this journey has produced. First, I would like to thank God for giving me the vision and desire to write and complete this devotional. Secondly, I would like to thank my family and friends who read every word and provided feedback to improve this work from God. I could only have done this with them. I would also like to highlight my parents, who were the first to instill God's Word in me. I thank my brother, who pushes my thinking, and my wife and child, who continuously help me see God's love each day. Thank you, and God bless.

BOOK DESCRIPTION

For two years after his mother's death, Justin Simmons struggled with the concept of His personal relationship with God. As a result, it affected how he interacted with his faith and family. So much so that he disregarded well-intentioned messages from the people he loved; instead, he blamed, questioned, and despised the Almighty for what had transpired.

After a critical conversation with the Creator, Justin shifted his perspective, discovered who he was, and found empowerment through the stories of Jesus Christ. The devotional, *Live By the Word: The ABCs of Life and Messages for the Soul,* is a manifestation of Justin's journey and how he was able to reconnect, transform, and prosper in every aspect of his life. The goal of this work is for others to do the same and to have a guide in strengthening their relationships with themselves, others, and the Lord.